The Story of a Special Day
Volume 360

December
25

December 25 is the 359th day of the year (360th in leap years).
There are 6 days remaining until the end of the year.

by Michael Dobson

Timespinner
Press

This book is also available in e-book form for Kindle, e-pub devices, and other formats from your favorite online booksellers.

For more information about the series, about us, or about your special day, please email us at editor@timespinnerpress.com.

Look for other volumes in *The Story of a Special Day,* coming often. See www.timespinnerpress.com for details and for the most recent information.

Table of Contents

**For the definition of "O.S.," "N.S.," "CE," and "BCE" used
with some dates , see the section "On Names and Dates."**

Cover: Santa Claus, from the cover of the December 3, 1902 issue
of *Puck* Magazine.

Quote of the Day

"Maybe Christmas," he thought, "doesn't come from a store. Maybe Christmas...perhaps...means a little bit more."

from *How the Grinch Stole Christmas!*
by Dr. Seuss (Theodor Seuss Geisel)

Today in History

December 25

"Merry Old Santa Claus" by Thomas Nast, from the January 1, 1881, edition of *Harper's Weekly.*

Event of the Day
Christmas

Throughout the world, December 25 is celebrated as Christmas Day, a celebration commemorating the birth of Jesus. Because Christmas has both religious and secular aspects, it is a public holiday in many nations, celebrated by most Christians and many non-Christians alike.

A Brief History of Christmas

The New Testament does not give any specific date for the birth of Jesus, and unlike Easter, Christmas was not observed by the early church. The first recorded celebration of Christmas in the western Christian tradition doesn't appear until 336 CE*. In the eastern Christian tradition, the feast of the Epiphany (January 6 in the Gregorian calendar), commemorating the baptism of Jesus, was celebrated instead.

Scholars disagree on the reason December 25 was chosen. One argument is that December 25 was already celebrated in Rome as the *Dies Natalis Solis Invicti* ("birthday of the Unconquered Sun"), and when Christianity became the official religion of the Roman Empire, the goal was to Christianize this pagan holiday.

---

* For the definition of "CE" and other abbreviations associated with dates, see "On Names and Dates."

Others argue that the choice of December 25 was based on the date of the Annunciation, the celebration of the angel Gabriel's announcement to the Virgin Mary that she would become the mother of Jesus. Christmas, by that tradition, was to be celebrated exactly nine months after that date.

It's also the case that many nations and religions had a major feast on or about December 25. This is because the Winter Solstice (shortest day of the year in the Northern Hemisphere and longest in the Southern Hemisphere) takes place somewhere between the 20th and 22nd day of December. By the 25th, it was clear that the days were once again getting longer, hence the connection with the Sun.

Whatever the reason, Epiphany, not Christmas, was the major Christian celebration of the time. Slowly, however, the status of Christmas grew. The Emperor Charlemagne was crowned on Christmas Day, 800 CE, as were English Kings Edmund the Martyr (855 CE) and William the Conqueror (1066 CE). In 1377 CE, King Richard II celebrated Christmas with a feast in which 28 oxen and 300 sheep were eaten.

Although the December 25 date was now customarily associated with the birth of Jesus, the medieval version of Christmas was associated with the Twelve Days of Christmas, rather than with a single day. Gift-giving, for example, was normally done on New Year's Day.

Christmas in the Middle Ages wasn't particularly child-friendly. The "Feast of Fools" was part of the holiday season, with a "Lord of Misrule" presiding

"A Christmas Carol," Dante Gabriel Rossetti (1867)

over an orgy of drunkenness, promiscuity, and gambling.

This is why some Christian denominations, especially the Puritans, objected to the the celebration of Christmas altogether. In 1647 CE, Christmas was banned in England, and in spite of public protests, the holiday was not restored until 1660. In Scotland, Christmas didn't become a public holiday again until 1958!

Puritans in the New World continued their opposition to Christmas. It was outlawed in Boston in 1659 and did not become legal again until 1681 — though Christmas didn't become popular again in the region until the mid 19th century! (German settlers in Pennsylvania, however, were always enthusiastic supporters of the holiday.)

We owe much of our modern view of Christmas to the 1822 poem "A Visit from St. Nicholas"(commonly known as "The Night Before Christmas") by Clement Clarke Moore and the 1843 novel *A Christmas Carol* by Charles Dickens. For the first time, children were at the center of the Christmas celebration. The popularity of gift-giving made Christmas an economically important season, though others saw it as corrupting the holiday's true meaning.

Because Christmas feasts and gifts cost money, Christmas was more often celebrated by the well-to-do rather than people of ordinary means. It wasn't until the 1950s when post-war prosperity brought the modern celebration of Christmas within the reach of most people. Today, the Christmas shopping season

An 1862 illustration by F. O. C. Darley from "A Visit from St.Nicholas" by Clement Clarke Moore

accounts for as much as a quarter of all personal spending in the US, although Christmas Day itself is the least active business day of the year, because most businesses are closed.

Christmas Traditions

Christmas traditions combine secular, pagan, and religious elements. Nativity scenes, religious services, and the singing of hymns come directly from Christianity. "Yule," as in the "Yuletide season" and the "yule log" date back to Nordic and German pagan traditions, as do such Christmas symbols as the Christmas tree, holly, and mistletoe.

Christmas decorations date back until at least the 15th century, and nativity displays are known to have existed as early as 10th century Rome.

Many traditional songs of Christmas are clearly religious in nature, but secular songs ranging from "Deck the Halls" to "Jingle Bells" and "Grandma Got Run Over by a Reindeer" are also strongly associated with the holiday.

Christmas cards, both religious and secular, first make their appearance in 1843, and by the turn of the century were increasingly popular. In 2005, 1.9 billion Christmas cards were sent in the US alone!

The first commercial Christmas card, published by Sir Henry Cole in 1843

Christmas feasts are also traditional, but the food consumed varied by country. In the US, it's traditionally turkey. In Sicily, twelve kinds of fish are served. The English traditionally cook goose, the Swedish serve a smörgåsbord including ham, meatballs and herring.

Christmas desserts are popular, from the

traditional "bring me some figgy pudding" to the Maltese *Imbuljuta tal-Qastan*, the French *bûche de Noël*, the Italian *panettone*, the German *stollen*, and Jamaican run fruit cake. Eggnog (with or without booze) is popular in many nations.

Who brings the Christmas gifts also varies. Many cultures mention St. Nicholas, a 4th century bishop of a city in what is now Turkey, because he was noted for caring for children and for the giving of gifts. St, Nicholas is variously known as Father Christmas, Santa Claus, Sinterklaas, Père Noël, Joulupukki, Babbo Natale, and Ded Moroz. In Germany, the *Christkind* (Christ child) brings the gifts; in Scandinavia a Christmas gnome known as *tomte* does the job.

While traditionally St. Nicholas was portrayed as wearing bishop's robes and hat, the modern popular portrayal of Santa Claus is primarily the work of American cartoonist Thomas Nast, who drew an annual image of Santa Claus each year beginning in 1863. Advertisers (most famously Coca-Cola) adapted the Nast figure into the jolly bearded figure we know today.

Christmas Around the World

Not everyone celebrates Christmas on December 25. Many parts of the Eastern Orthodox Church celebrate on January 7, instead. In the older Julian calendar†, used by Orthodox "Old Calendrists,"

---

† See "On Names and Dates."

December 25 is the same as January 7 in Gregorian reckoning. The Armenian Apostolic Church does not celebrate the birth of Jesus as a separate holiday, but celebrates the birth and baptism (Theophany) together on January 6, a public holiday in Armenia. A spinoff, the Armenian Patriarchate of Jerusalem celebrates January 6, but uses the Julian calendar, which is the equivalent of January 19 on the Gregorian calendar.

No matter which date you celebrate, or which tradition you use, the Christmas virtues of neighborliness, kindness, and charity are worth honoring.

That is, as soon as you've finished opening your presents.

Christmas Morning, by Carl Larsson (1894)

Detail from *Washington Crossing the Delaware,* by Emanuel Leutze

What Happened on December 25?

From the creation of great works of engineering and art, to devastating wars and natural disasters, thousands of years of history have left their mark on each and every day of the year. Here are some important events that occurred on December 25. (Items with a photo or illustration are boxed.)

1492 — **The *Santa María*,** one of the three ships in Christopher Columbus's expedition to the New World, **sinks** after running aground on a reef near Haiti the previous day.

1643 — **Christmas Island**, now an external territory of Australia, **is discovered** and named by British captain William Mynors, who sailed by the island without landing.

1776 — The Continental Army, commanded by General George **Washington, crosses the Delaware** River at night to attack British Hessian forces in Trenton, New Jersey.

1826 — The **Eggnog Riot** at the United States Military Academy at West Point, New York, a drunken party which began the previous evening, ends.

1831 — The **Great Jamaican Slave Revolt,** also known as the **Christmas Rebellion,** led by black Baptist preacher Samuel Sharpe, begins. It will eventually involve 60,000 slaves and last eleven days before being brutally put down by British and Jamaican government forces and plantation owners. British reaction to the brutality is thought to have influenced the abolishment of slavery, which took place some seven years later.

1837 — In the **Battle of Lake Okeechobee**, 800 US troops commanded by Colonel (later President) Zachary Taylor, battle around 400 Seminole Indians resisting forced relocation. The engagement is regarded as a tactical Seminole victory, but by 1858 the Seminoles were defeated and Florida ceded to the US.

1868 — President Andrew Johnson issues a proclamation granting **full pardon and amnesty to Confederate soldiers**.

1914 — A series of unofficial ceasefires spontaneously break out along the Western Front of World War I in what became known as the **Christmas Truce**. French, German, and British soldiers crossed trenches to exchange holiday greetings, swap food and souvenirs, and play football (soccer).

1926 — Following the death of his father, **Prince Hirohito of Japan ascends the Chrysanthemum Throne** to become the Shōwa Emperor (昭和天皇), reigning until his death in 1989.

Photograph of British and German soldiers playing football (soccer)
during the Christmas Truce, 1914

1950 — Four Scottish students **steal the Stone of Scone** (also known as the Coronation Stone for its ceremonial role in the coronation of British monarchs) from Westminster Abbey. It is broken in the process, and the pieces are recovered the following year.

1968 — The **Apollo 8** mission, the first manned spacecraft to leave Earth orbit, leaves its orbit around the Moon to begin its journey back to Earth. Its Christmas message, delivered the previous evening, is one of the memorable moments of that mission.

1991 — **Mikhail Gorbachev** (Михаил Горбачёв) **steps down as President of the Soviet Union.** The Soviet Union itself officially dissolved the following day.

Quote of the Day

"If I have seen further it is by standing on the sholders of Giants."

Sir Isaac Newton, physicist and mathematician
born December 25, 1642

Births
and
Deaths

December 25

Sir Isaac Newton, based on a painting by Sir Godfrey Keller.
Newton was born December 25, 1642

Notable December 25 People

With the current world population at about seven billion people, on average about 19 million people also celebrate their birthdays on December 25 — and that isn't counting millions and millions who came before! No matter when you were born, you share your birthday with many special people whose accomplishments (and occasionally embarrassments) have been noted as part of history.

In this section, you'll meet fascinating people who share your birthday. They're organized by what they're famous for, and then in reverse chronological order from most recent to earliest. Those who are shown in photographs or artwork have a box around them. We don't have photos of everyone, so please forgive us if your favorite person is missing.

Some of these people you've heard of, others will be new to you, but they all make up an important part of the reason that December 25 is a truly special day!

Louis Chevrolet (Courtesy George Grantham Bain Collection, Library of Congress)

Who Was Born on December 25?

Business

Zora Arkus-Duntov, automobile designer known as the "father of the Corvette." *(1909)*

Glenn McCarthy, oil tycoon who founded Houston's Shamrock Hotel, inspired the fictional character Jeff Rink in the 1952 Edna Ferber novel *Giant,* made into a 1956 film with James Dean playing Rink. *(1907)*

Lew Grade, British media proprietor and impressario who founded ITC, which produced *The Muppet Show, The Prisoner,* and various Gerry Anderson "Supermarionation" series such as *Thunderbirds.* (1906)

Lila Bell Wallace, magazine publisher who co-founded *Reader's Digest* magazine. *(1889)*

Conrad Hilton, hotelier who founded the Hilton Hotels chain. *(1887)*

Louis Chevrolet, race-car driver who founded the Chevrolet Motor Car Company, named to the International Motorsports Hall of Fame. *(1878)*

Entertainment

C. C. H. Pounder, actress known for her roles in *The Shield, Warehouse 13, Sons of Anarchy,* and *NCIS: New Orleans. (1952)*

Sissy Spacek, actress first famous for *Carrie,* won an Academy Award for *Coal Miner's Daughter. (1949)*

Gary Sandy, actor best known as program director Andy Travis on the late 1970s sitcom *WKRP in Cincinnati. (1945)*

Rick Berman, succeeded Gene Roddenberry as executive producer and manager of the *Star Trek* franchise; produced several of the spin-off series as well as films. *(1945)*

Ismail Merchant, film producer known for his long partnership with James Ivory as Merchant Ivory Productions, whose films won six Academy Awards. *(1936)*

Mabel King, actress who played "Mama" on the 1970s sitcom *What's Happening!* and Evillene the Witch in the musical and film *The Wiz. (1932)*

Rod Serling, screenwriter and television producer primarily known for creating *The Twilight Zone. (1924)*

Quentin Crisp, English writer and raconteur whose 1968 autobiography *The Naked Civil Servant* was adapted into film. *(1908)*

Rod Serling

Mike Mazurki, professional writer turned actor, best known for tough-guy roles. *(1907)*

Humphrey Bogart, iconic actor whose best known films include *The Maltese Falcon* and *Casablanca*. *(1899)*

Robert Ripley, cartoonist and entrepreneur who created Ripley's Believe It or Not!, which began as a newspaper cartoon but expanded into radio, television, and a series of museums known as "Odditoriums." *(1890)*

A 1944 *Believe It or Not!* cartoon

Humphrey Bogart

Fashion

Helena Christensen, Victoria's Secret fashion model who appeared in the music video for the Chris Isaak song "Wicked Game." *(1968)*

Helena Rubinstein, cosmetics entrepreneur who became one of the world's richest women. *(1872)*

Government and Military

Justin Trudeau, prime minister of Canada, son of former prime minister Pierre Trudeau. *(1971)*

Karl Rove, political consultant and advisor who served as deputy chief of staff to President George W. Bush, political analyst and contributor to Fox News, *The Wall Street Journal,* and other media. *(1950)*

Anwar Sadat (أنور السادات), President of Egypt until his assassination, shared the Nobel Peace Prize with Israeli President Menachem Begin for their work on the Camp David Accords. *(1918)*

Muhammad Ali Jinnah (محمد علی جناح), leader in the Indian independence movement, founder of the state of Pakistan and served as first Governor-General, known as *Quaid-i-Azam* ("Great Leader") and *Baba-i-Qaum* ("Father of the Nation"). *(1876)*

Philip Mazzei, Italian physician and friend of Thomas Jefferson, secret agent and arms dealer for Virginia during and after the American Revolution. *(1730)*

Anwar Sadat (Courtesy *US News and World Report* Collection,
Library of Congress)

Heroism and Adventure

Michael P. Anderson, USAF officer and astronaut who perished in the Space Shuttle *Columbia* disaster in 2003. *(1959)*

Noël Leslie, Countess of Rothes, socialite and philanthropist who became a heroine of the *Titanic* disaster for taking the tiller of her lifeboat and helping row it to safety. *(1878)*

Medicine

Adolf Windaus, won the 1928 Nobel Prize in Chemistry for his work on sterols and their relation to vitamins. *(1876)*

Clara Barton, hospital nurse known as the "Angel of the Battlefield" during the American Civil War; founded the American Red Cross. *(1821)*

Music

Josh Freese, drummer for the Vandals, Devo, Nine Inch Nails, Guns N' Roses, and other bands. *(1972)*

Dido, singer-songwriter whose 1999 debut album *No Angel* sold over 21 million copies worldwide, nominated for an Academy Award for the song "If I Rise." *(1971)*

Clara Barton (Photo: Mathew Brady)

Alannah Myles, singer-songwriter whose 1990 single "Black Velvet" won the Grammy Award for Best Female Rock Vocal Performance. *(1958)*

Steve Wariner, country singer-songwriter who has had more than 50 singles on the *Billboard* Country Music Charts. *(1954)*

Annie Lennox, singer-songwriter best known as a member of the Eurythmics, known for such hits as "Sweet Dreams (Are Made of This)." *(1954)*

Barbara Mandrell, country musician and member of the Country Music Hall of Fame, hosted tthe 1980s variety show *Barbara Mandrell and the Mandrell Sisters*, known for such songs as "(If Loving You is Wrong) I Don't Want to be Right" and "I Was Country When Country Wasn't Cool." *(1948)*

Jimmy Buffett, musician known for such songs as "Margaritaville," "Come Monday," and "Cheeseburger in Paradise." *(1946)*

Noel Redding, rock bassist and guitarist best known as the bassist with the Jimi Hendrix Experience. *(1945)*

Pete Brown, lyricist and singer best known for his collaborations with Cream, including "White Room" and "Sunshine of Your Love." *(1940)*

Enrique Jorrín, Cuban violinist who invented the cha-cha-chá. *(1926)*

Cab Calloway, jazz singer and bandleader whose best-known song was "Minnie the Moocher." *(1907)*

Cab Calloway (Photo: William P. Gottlieb)

Evelyn Nesbit (Photo: Gertrude Käsebier)

William Bell, classical tuba player and educator who developed the Bell method. *(1902)*

Kid Ory, New Orleans jazz trombonist and bandleader popular in the 1910s and 1920s. *(1886)*

Patrick Gilmore, composer and bandleader best known for writing the lyrics to "When Johnny Comes Marching Home Again." *(1829)*

Scandal

Evelyn Nesbit, chorus girl, model, and actress immortalized by architect Stanford White as "The Girl in the Red Velvet Swing." Her jealous husband, Harry Kendall Thaw, shot and killed White, leading to what was then referred to as the "Trial of the Century." *(1884)*

Science and Technology

Ernst Ruska, designed the first electron microscope, won the 1986 Nobel Prize in Physics. *(1906)*

Gerhard Herzberg, won the 1971 Nobel Prize in Chemistry for his contributions to understanding the electronic structure and geometry of molecules. *(1904)*

L. L. Langstroth, American clergyman and beekeeper who created the modern day movable frame beehive, considered the "father of American beekeeping." *(1810)*

Jairzinho (Photo: Rob Mieremet, courtesy Dutch National Archives)

Claude Chappe, inventor who developed a semaphore system that eventually covered all of French, considered the first practical telecommunications system of the industrial age. *(1763)*

Sir Isaac Newton, one of the most influential and important scientists in history. *(1642 [N.S.‡ January 4, 1643]) (Photo page 16)*

Sports

Rickey Henderson, left fielder nicknamed "The Man of Steal," inducted into the Baseball Hall of Fame. *(1958)*

Larry Csonka, fullback for the Miami Dolphins and other teams, member of the Pro Football Hall of Fame. *(1946)*

Ken Stabler, football quarterback named to the Pro Football Hall of Fame in 2016. *(1945)*

Jairzinho, Brazilian footballer (soccer player), listed on World Soccer Magazine's list of the 100 greatest players of the 20th century. *(1944)*

Françoise Dürr, tennis player ranked in the world top ten for six years, with a career high of World No. 3; inducted into the International Tennis Hall of Fame. *(1942)*

---

‡ See "On Names and Dates."

Nellie Fox, second baseman for the Philadelphia Athletics, the Chicago White Sox, and the Houston Astros; member of the Baseball Hall of Fame. *(1927)*

Clarrie Grimmett, cricketer credited with the development of the flipper, member of the Australian Cricket Hall of Fame and the ICC Cricket Hall of Fame. *(1891)*

Samuel Berger, American pugilist who won a gold medal in boxing at the 1904 Summer Olympics, member of the International Jewish Sports Hall of Fame. *(1884)*

Thomas W. Cahill, one of the founding fathers of soccer (football) in the United States, member of the US National Soccer Hall of Fame. *(1864)*

Pud Galvin, baseball pitcher who became the first 300-game winner in MLB history, inducted into the Baseball Hall of Fame. *(1856)*

Writing

Carlos Castaneda, author, anthropologist, and mystic whose adventures with Yaqui Indian mystic Don Juan resulted in a series of best selling books. *(1925)*

Pud Galvin

Charlie Chaplin, from the film *A Dog's Life* (1918)

Who Died on December 25?

Art

Joan Miró, Spanish painter and sculptor known for his surrealist paintings. *(1983)*

Entertainment

Denver Pyle, actor best known for playing patriarch Jesse Duke on the television series *The Dukes of Hazzard. (1997)*

Dean Martin, singer and actor known for his partnership with Jerry Lewis, as a member of the famed "Rat Pack," and for such hits as "That's Amore" and "Everybody Loves Somebody." *(1995)*

Joan Blondell, actress who appeared in over 100 films, nominated for an Academy Award for 1951's *The Blue Veil,* known to modern audiences for her role as Vi in 1978's *Grease. (1979)*

Charlie Chaplin, actor and filmmaker, iconic figure of the silent film era. *(1977)*

Leon Schlesinger, founded an animation company later acquired by Warner Brothers, producer of the *Looney Tunes* and *Merrie Melodies* cartoons starring such characters as Bugs Bunny and Daffy Duck. *(1949)*

W. C. Fields, comedian and actor known for his cynical, hard-drinking comic persona, famous for such quotes as "Never give a sucker an even break." *(1946)*

Government and Military

Nicolae Ceaușescu, Communist dictator of Romania, executed with his wife Elena in the aftermath of the Romanian Revolution. *(1989)*

Samuel de Champlain, French explorer known as the "father of New France" for founding Quebec. *(1635)*

Music

Eartha Kitt, singer and actress whose hits include "C'est Si Bon" and "Santa Baby," played Catwoman in the 1960s television series *Batman*. *(2008)*

James Brown, singer-songwriter known as the "Godfather of Soul," whose hits include "Papa's Got a Brand New Bag" and "I Got You (I Feel Good)." *(2006)*

Birgit Nilsson, Swedish operatic soprano, considered one of the greatest of the 20th century. *(2005)*

W. C. Fields, from the film *David Copperfield* (1935)

Science and Technology

Gabriel Voisin, French aviation pioneer, founded Voisin, the world's first commercial airplane factory. *(1973)*

Otto Loewi, pharmacologist and psychobiologist who shared the 1936 Nobel Prize in Physiology or Medicine for discovering acetylcholine. *(1961)*

Linus Yale, Jr., American engineer who invented the cylinder lock and built the Yale Lock Manufacturing Company, member of the National Inventors Hall of Fame. *(1868)*

Religion

Saint Albert Chmielowski, Polish saint canonized for founding the Albertine Brothers and Sisters *(1916)*

Sports

Wally Ris, American swimmer who won two Olympic gold medals, member of the International Swimming Hall of Fame. *(1989)*

Billy Martin, manager of the New York Yankees known for his temper and his tumultuous relationship with Yankees owner George Steinbrenner. *(1989)*

Young Tom Morris, Scottish golfer who helped pioneer professional golf. *(1875)*

Writing

George Clayton Johnson, science fiction writer known as co-author of the novel *Logan's Run,* adapted into a 1976 film, and for scripts for *The Twilight Zone* and Star Trek; also wrote the story on which the 1960 and 2001 films *Ocean's Eleven* were based. *(2015)*

Karel Čapek,Czech writer best known for the play *R.U.R. (Rossum's Universal Robots),* which introduced the word "robot" to the world, nominated seven times for the Nobel Prize in Literature. *(1938)*

Old Tom Morris (left) and **Young Tom Morris** (right)

Quote of the Day

"I cook with wine, and sometimes I even add it to the food."

W. C. Fields, actor and comedian, died December 25, 1946

Holidays
Around
the World

December 25

The Sol Invictus temple in Rome, by Hermann Bender (1879)

Holidays Around the World

If you're looking for a reason to take your special day off, you should know that every single day is a holiday somewhere in the world! Here's some of what you can celebrate on December 25!

General Events

Children's Day (numerous African nations)

Many nations set aside a day each year to celebrate children. In the African nations of Cameroon, Central African Republic, Chad, Equatorial Guinea, Democratic Republic of the Congo, Gabon, and the Republic of Congo, Children's Day comes on Christmas each year.

Constitution Day (行憲紀念日) (Taiwan/Republic of China)

Many nations set aside a day each year to commemorate their constitution. In Taiwan, the date honors the 1947 anniversary of the Republic of China Constitution.

Dies Natalis of Sol Invictus (ancient Rome)

Sol Invictus ("Unconquered Sun") was the official sun god of the late Roman empire, and had his official feast day on December 25.

Good Governance Day (सुशासन दविस) (India)

Good Governance Day in India commemorates the birth anniversary of Prime Minister Atal Bihari Vajpayee and fosters awareness among Indian peole of accountability in government.

Malkh Festival (Nakh people of Chechnya and Ingushetia)

Among the Nakh people, December 25 is the birthday and festival of the Sun, dedicated to the Deela-Malkh in Vainakh mythology.

Newtonmas (Atheists)

Rather than celebrate Christmas, some atheists observe December 25 as Newtonmas, the birthday of Sir Isaac Newton.

Quaid-e-Azam Day (Pakistan)

In Pakistan, the birthday of founder Muhammad Ali Jinnah (known as "Quaid-e-Azam," or "Great Leader) is celebrated on December 25.

Takanakuy (Chumbivilcas Province, Peru)

Takanakuy ("to hit each other" in Quechua), is an annual festival held on December 25, in which individuals fight one another to settle old conflicts or to display their manhood. People dress in costumes reflecting Andean cultural symbols, and in addition to the fighting there is much drinking (to numb the pain) and dancing.

Food Holidays

In the United States, almost every day of the year is dedicated to a particular food. (Some other countries also have official food days, but only in America is there one every single day!) Sponsored by manufacturers, retailers, farmers, or simply fans, these days are often proclaimed by the President, Congress, state governors, or mayors. Given that there are more different foods than days of the year, some days honor more than one kind of food!

In the US, December 25 is **National Pumpkin Pie Day.** Pumpkin pie is a relatively recent invention. American colonists used pumpkin in pie crusts, but not in the filling. What we think of a modern pumpkin pie didn't exist until the 1700s. According to Foodimentary, it's also **National "Kiss the Cook" Day**, in gratitude for a great Christmas dinner

In addition, the entire month of December is used to celebrate numerous foods. With Christmas on the horizon, it shouldn't be surprising that December is **National Egg Nog Month** and **National Fruit Cake Month**. You can wash down your pumpkin pie with some egg nog, and treat your cook to some fruit cake!

And while we're on the subject of food, it's also **Food Service Safety Month**. The first week in December is also **National Handwashing Week**, which is clearly related to food safety.

Religious Feast Days and Holidays

Hanukkah (חֲנֻכָּה) (Judaism)

The Jewish celebration of Hanukkah, also known as the Festival of Lights or the Feast of Dedication, takes place for eight days and nights beginning on the 25th day of Kislev, which varies from late November to late December. It commemorates the rededication of the Second Temple in Jerusalem at the time of the Maccabean Revolt.

Each night of Hanukkah is marked by lighting one branch of the Menorah, a candelabrum with nine branches. In addition to prayers, celebrants eat foods fried or baked in olive oil. Children play with a spinning top known as a dreidel and receive Hanukkah gelt.

18th century painting of a Hanukkah celebration, artist unknown.

Saint Days
Each day in the year is considered a feast day for one or more saints. They are somewhat different in western Christianity (Catholicism and many forms of Protestantism) and in eastern (Orthodox) Christianity. There are many others; this is a selection.

In *Western Christianity*, December 25 is not only the occasion of the Nativity, but it is also the feast day of Anastasia of Sirmium.

In *Eastern Orthodox Christianity*, it is also the commemoration of Eugenia of Rome, Adalsindis, and Æthelburh of Wilton. (These people are honored on January 7 by "Old Calendrists.")

Honorary Months

Presidents, Congresses, and nations around the world issue proclamations recognizing particular months to honor certain causes. These events generally fall in December, though honorary months do come and go. Holidays established by states and nonprofit organizations are listed if verified. If not otherwise specified, all months are US. There is some variation from year to year; some celebratory months get added and others get dropped. Two places to get up to date information are the current edition of *Chase's Calendar of Events* or the website Brownielocks. Here are some honorary designations for December.

- Bingo's Birthday Month (the game, not the dog)

- National Critical Infrastructure Protection Month
- National Impaired Driving Prevention Month
- National Sign Up for Summer Camp Month
- National Stress-Free Family Holiday Month
- Safe Toys and Gifts Month
- Spiritual Literacy Month
- Universal Human Rights Month
- Write a Business Plan Month

Moveable and Multi-Day Events

Some events take place over a specific week or time period. Start and finish dates may vary from year to year. Some events occur on different days each year (such as "fourth Saturday of a month"). These events sometimes take place on December 25.

Last Friday in December (December 25-31)
- Children's Day (Dominica)

Bingo card (Photo: Abbey Hendrickson, CC BY-SA 2.0) — for
BINGO'S BIRTHDAY MONTH

Quote of the Day

"Ooh, with a little luck —
December will be magic again."

Kate Bush, singer-songwriter
"December Will be Magic Again"

About
the
Month
of

December

THEM
ACC
MAGNA

"December," from the *Brevarium Grimani* by Simon Bening (c.1510)

December: The Twelfth Month

"In cold December fragrant chaplets blow,
And heavy harvests nod beneath the snow."

— Alexander Pope, *Dunciad*.

In Latin, *decem* means "ten," so it may seem strange that December is actually the twelfth month of the year. The original Roman calendar, from which our month names come, began in March, making December indeed the tenth month.

No one is completely sure when the start of the year was moved to January, but the traditional name of December stuck.

In the northern hemisphere, December is the month with the shortest daylight hours of the year; in the southern hemisphere, it's the opposite. December is the equivalent of June in the southern hemisphere, and vice versa.

In the Julian and Gregorian calendars, December is the twelfth and last month of the year, and is one of seven months with 31 days.

In every year, December starts on the same day of the week as September, and ends on the same day of the week as April.

The length of the day varies through the year, because the Earth tilts as it revolves around the Sun. The two extremes are known as the *solstices*, and the points at which day and night are of equal length are known as the *equinoxes*. The northern hemisphere's winter solstice, which is the shortest day of the year, falls in December. In the southern hemisphere, the summer solstice, the longest day of the year, falls in December.

The dates of the solstice can vary between December 20 and 22. Because even the ancients could tell when the days stopped getting shorter (or longer) and started in the other direction, many holidays and festivals take place around the time of the solstice, including most famously Christmas.

"December," by Gabriel Perelle

December in Other Cultures

In Albanian, the month of December is known as *Dhjetor*. In Egyptian Arabic, it's ديسمبر (pronounced *dīsambar*). In Czech, it's *Prosinec*, in Finland it's *Joulukuu*, and in Poland it's *Grudzień*. Hungarians say *Karácsony hava*.

In Greek, the month of Δεκέμβριος is pronounced *Dekémbrios*. In Hebrew, it's דצמבר and Hindi, it's दिसंबर.

In Irish Gaelic, the month of December is *Nollaig mi na Nollag* and in Scottish Gaelic it's *an Dùbhlachd*. The Welsh say *Rhagfyr*.

The Chinese and Japanese both write the month 十二月, but it is pronounced differently in Cantonese, Mandarin, and Japanese. Koreans write it as 십이월, or *Sipiweol*. In Vietnam it's 朓迸罢 (*Tháng mười hai*).

In Old English, the month is *Gēolmōnaþ* and in Anglo-Saxon it's *Ærra-ġēola mōnaþ*.

The month of December does not correspond exactly with months in other calendar systems. The Hebrew months of כִּסְלֵו (*Kislev*) and טֵבֵת (*Tevet*) overlap December, as do the Persian months of آذر (*Azar*) and دی (*Dey*) and the Hindu months of मार्गशीर्ष (*Mārgaśirṣa*) and पूस (*Pauṣa*).

In the Islamic world, the lunar calendar consists of 354 or 355 days, meaning that the months slowly migrate through the year, and over time different months correspond to December.

How to Say "Merry Christmas and Happy New Year" in Many Languages

Albanian: Gëzuar Krishtlindjet dhe Vitin e Ri

Basque: Gabon Zoriontsuak eta urte berri on

Breton: Nedeleg laouen na bloavezh mat

Bulgarian: Весела Коледа и Честита Нова Година

Catalan: Bon Nadal i Feliç Any Nou

Chinese Simplified (China, except Hong Kong): 圣诞快乐，新年进步

Chinese Traditional (Hong Kong & Taiwan): 聖誕快樂，新年進步

Cornish: Nadelik Lowen, Bledhen Nowyth Da.

Croatian: Hrvatski: Čestit Božić i sretna Nova godina

Czech: Veselé vánoce a šťastný nový rok.(More common is "P.F," which stands for *Pour féliciter* (a French phrase meaning"For happiness in the year.").

Danish: Glædelig jul og godt nytår! or simply God jul

Dutch: Prettige kerstdagen en een gelukkig nieuwjaar

Estonian: Häid jõule ja head uut aastat

Esperanto: Gajan kristnaskon kaj feliĉan novan jaron

Filipino: Maligayang Pasko at Manigong Bagong Taon

Finnish: Hyvää joulua ja onnellista uutta vuotta

French: Joyeux Noël et Bonne Année

Galician: Bo Nadal e Feliz Aninovo

Georgian: გილოცავთ შობა-ახალ წელს

German: Fröhliche Weihnachten und ein glückliches/gutes Neues Jahr

Greek: Καλά Χριστούγεννα και ευτυχισμένος ο Καινούριος Χρόνος

Hungarian: Kellemes karácsonyi ünnepeket és boldog új évet or simply "B. ú. é. k."

Icelandic: Gleðileg jól og farsælt nýtt ár

Indonesian: Selamat Hari Natal dan Tahun Baru

Irish: Nollaig Shona Duit

Italian: Buon Natale e Felice Anno Nuovo

Korean: 메리 크리스마스

Japanese: メリー・クリスマス

Latvian: Priecīgus Ziemassvētkus un laimīgu Jauno gadu

Lithuanian: Linksmų šventų Kalėdų ir laimingų Naujųjų metų

Macedonian: Среќна Нова Година и честит Божиќ

Malay: Selamat Hari Krismas dan Tahun Baru

Maltese: Il-Milied Hieni u s-Sena t-Tajba

Mongolian: Зул сар болон Шинэ жилийн баярын мэнд хүргье

Norwegian: God jul og godt nyttår

Persian: کریسمس و سال نو مبارک

Polish: Wesołych Świąt i Szczęśliwego Nowego Roku

Portuguese: Feliz Natal e um Feliz Ano Novo

Romanian: Crăciun Fericit și La mulți ani

Russian: С Новым годом и Рождеством Христовым!

Sinhala: Suba naththalak wewa, suba aluth aurudhak wewa

Slovak: Veselé Vianoce a Šťastný Nový rok

Spanish: Feliz Navidad y próspero Año Nuevo

Swedish: God Jul och Gott Nytt År

Vietnamese: Chúc mừng Giáng Sinh và chúc mừng năm mơi (acute accent over ơ in "mơi")

Ukrainian: Веселих свят! (Happy Holidays!) / З Новим роком і Різдвом Христовим!

Urdu: آپکو بڑا دن اور نیا سال مبارک ہو

Welsh: Nadolig Llawen a Blwyddyn Newydd Hapus

A Currier & Ives Christmas card, 1876

December Sayings and Superstitions

- "A green December fills the graveyard."
- "When December snows fall fast, marry and true love will last."
- "A December bride will be fond of novelty, entertaining but extravagant."
- "Married in days of December's cheer / Love's star shines brighter from year to year."

Which day should you marry? That's easy.

> "Monday for health
> Tuesday for wealth
> Wednesday best of all
> Thursday for losses
> Friday for crosses
> Saturday for no luck at all."

According to legend, auspicious dates for December weddings are 1, 8, 10, 19, 23, and 29.

December Symbols

Birthstone: December birthstones in various traditions include turquoise, lapiz lazuli, zircon, blue topaz, and tanzanite.

Oil painting on lapis lazuli, *Perseus Rescuing Andromeda*, by Giuseppe Cesari.

Birth Flowers: December's flowers are the
narcissus and the holly.

Illustration by Anton Hartinger from *Atlas der Alpenflora* (1882)

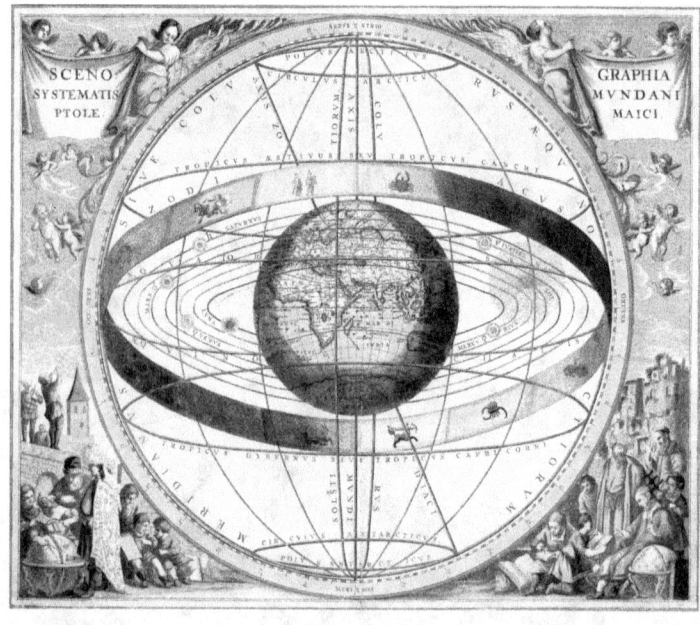

Scenography of the Ptolemaic Cosmography, by Johannes van Loon, based on Andreas Cellarius's *Harmonia Macrocosmica*, 1660

December 25 Zodiac Signs

From the perspective of someone on Earth, the Sun appears to move through the sky throughout the year, along a path astronomers call the *ecliptic plane*. The ecliptic plane is divided into twelve constellations, known as the zodiac, based on traditionally observed patterns of stars. On your birthday, you can't see your constellation, because it's in the daytime sky.

The zodiac was first developed by Babylonian astronomers about 2,500 years ago. Because they were unaware that the Earth wobbles like a spinning top (known as *precession*), they didn't make allowance for the fact that the Sun's path through the zodiac changes over time.

That means there are now two sets of dates for your birth sign. The *tropical dates* are the original Babylonian dates; the *sidereal dates* tell you where the Sun actually appears as it moves along its annual path.

For December 25, the tropical sign is **Capricorn** and the sidereal sign is **Sagittarius**.

Capricorn

Tropical December 22 to January 20
Sidereal January 15 to February 14

The origins of the constellation Capricorn date back
to Sumeria and Babylonia. Based on Enki, the
Sumerian god of wisdom and waters, Capricorn has
the head and upper body of a mountain goat and the
lower body and tail of a fish. The mountain goat
represents ambition and intelligence, the fish
represents passion and spirituality.

An earth sign, Capricorn is ruled by the planet
Saturn. They are often thought to be responsible,
patient, ambitious and loyal, but can sometimes be
seen as conceited, distrusting, and unimaginative.
Capricornians are supposed to be compatible with
Taurus, Pisces, and Virgo, but not with Aries,
Sagittarius, or Leo.

Sagittarius

Tropical November 23 to December 21
Sidereal December 16 to January 14

Sagittarius means "archer" in Latin. The constellation in the night sky is often depicted as having the appearance of a stick-figure archer drawing its bow.

The brighter stars in Sagittarius form an asterism known as The Teapot. The Milky Way is densest in Sagittarius, because the galactic center lies in that direction.

In astrology, Sagittarius is a fire sign. People born under it are said to be not superstitious. They are supposed to be drawn toward travel and philosophy, and to enjoy social contacts, meeting new people, and exploring other cultures. They are also said to be highly intelligent, visionary, and tolerant.

Sagittarians are considered compatible with Aries, Leo, and Gemini, and to a lesser extent with Taurus and Virgo.

Illustration by Edward Penfield

What Day of the Week is December 25?

On what day of the week does December 25 fall?

Surprisingly, this isn't an easy question. Because the calendar year is 365 days long (366 in leap years), it doesn't divide evenly by the seven days of the week.

Also, the Earth goes around the Sun in about 365-1/4 days, so a calendar tends to drift over time. That's why the same date falls on different weekdays in different years.

This is made even more complicated by a change in calendars that took place in 1582. Our modern calendar has its roots in ancient Rome, in a calendar reform conducted by Julius Caesar. Caesar commissioned mathematicians to attack the problem, and they came up with the idea of leap years, and thus standardized the calendar for centuries to come. This was called the Julian calendar.

Over time, however, the small errors in Caesar's calculation compounded. That's why Pope Gregory XIII commissioned the Gregorian calendar, used in most of the world today. Some countries converted in 1582, when the calendar was first developed; some converted later; other still haven't changed.

Gregorian and Julian aren't the only types of calendars. The Hebrew year, the Islamic year, and many other calendars are used in different parts of the world and among different people.

You can convert Gregorian dates to other calendars, including the Hebrew calendar, the Islamic calendar, and even the Mayan calendar by visiting the Fourmilab Calendar Converter at http://www.fourmilab.ch/documents/calendar/.

Chinese calendar systems are quite complex and have changed several times; a full discussion is far beyond the scope of this book. If you're interested, you can find information here: http://www.hermetic.ch/cal_stud/chinese_cal.htm.

On Names and Dates

Historians use "CE" (Common Era) and "BCE" (Before the Common Era) instead of the more common "AD" (Anno Domini, or Year of Our Lord) and "BC" (Before Christ), reflecting the fact that the year-numbering system established by the Gregorian calendar is used throughout the world in many countries not culturally Christian.

The CE/BCE designation dates back to at least 1708, and has been adopted as a standard by the United Nations and the Universal Postal Union. Because this series of books covers events and people of all nations and cultures, we use the CE/BCE terms.

The abbreviation "O.S." ("Old Style") and "N.S." ("New Style") on some dates refers to the fact that the Russian Empire (in particular) did not switch from the Julian to the Gregorian calendar at the same time as the rest of Europe, and therefore some figures and events have two dates.

Also, in the Julian calendar in England in the 16th century, the year began on March 25 rather than January 1. To avoid confusion with Gregorian dates, dates between January and March were often written using both years.

People and events whose original names are not in the Western alphabet have their native names (where possible) in the appropriate script shown in parenthesis. If you are using an e-reader to access an electronic version of this book, all characters don't always display on all devices.

A 50-year brass perpetual calendar.

Quote of the Day

"Time is an illusion, lunchtime doubly so."

Douglas Adams,
from *The Hitchhiker's Guide to the Galaxy*

Notes and Credits

Timespinner
Press

Cartoon by John T. McCutcheon

Copyright, Credit, and Contact

Follow Us

Our blog "This Day in History" (http://
timespinnerpress.com/this-day-in-history/) features short
articles on events and people associated with each day, and
updates several times each week. Also subscribe to the
"Quote of the Day" at http://timespinnerpress.com/quote-
of-the-day/. You can get daily links by following us on
Facebook at TimespinnerPress, or on Twitter as
@sidewisethinker.

Contact Us

Find an error or a format problem? Want information about
the series, about us, or about when the volume for your
special day might be available? Please email us at
editor@timespinnerpress.com. (We also take requests if your
special day isn't yet complete. Please give us at least six
weeks' notice if possible.)

Sources

We owe a great debt to Wikipedia, which is our first stop for
research. We attempt to make independent confirmation of
all important dates and facts through a variety of other
sources.

Other sources we frequently use include the Library of
Congress; "on this day" listings from *Encyclopedia Britannica*,
the *New York Times*, and the BBC; Omniglot for the names of
months in other languages; *Chase's Calendar of Events*; and, of
course, the always essential Google.

All art and photographs are either in the public domain, used under a Creative Commons license, or with a "fair use" justification, and most frequently come from Wikimedia Commons and the Library of Congress Prints and Photographs Division.

Attribution is provided where possible, or as requested by the copyright owner, or when there is particular historical significance, listed below. For information about any particular illustration or photograph, please contact us.

Credits

1. The image of Santa Claus on the cover originally appeared on the cover of the December 3, 1902 issue of *Puck* magazine (v. 52, no. 1344). It is in the public domain because its copyright has expired. The image is from the Library of Congress Prints and Photographs Division, digital ID ppmsca.25693.

2. The illustration of the month of December used on the back cover is from the French Gothic illuminated manuscript *Les Très Riches Heures du duc de Berry* by the Limbourg Brothers, Jean Colombe, and an intermediate painter whose name is lost to history. It is in the public domain because its copyright has expired.

3. The box graphic used on the first page is from a 1916 pamphlet entitled "Divorce versus Democracy" authored by G. K. Chesterton, originally published in London by the Society of St. Peter and St. Paul. It is in the public domain in the US because it was published prior to 1923, and is in the public domain in all countries (including the country of origin) in which the copyright time is the author's life plus 70 years or less.

4. The graphic design for the section pages in this book is from a design originally created for a pharmacy label. It is courtesy of Wellcome Images (ICV No 11073, photo V0010813), and is used here under CC BY-SA 4.0.

5. The 1881 drawing "Merry Old Santa Claus" by Thomas Nast is in the public domain because its copyright has expired.

6. The 1867 painting *A Christmas Carol* by Dante Gabriel Rossetti is in the public domain because its copyright has expired.

7. The 1862 illustration from "A Visit from St. Nicholas" is by F.O.C. Darley, and is courtesy of Project Gutenberg. It is in the public domain because its copyright has expired.

8. The first commercial Christmas card was published in 1843 by Sir Henry Cole, and is in the public domain because its copyright has expired.

9. The 1894 painting *Christmas Morning* by Carl Larsson is in the public domain because its copyright has expired.

10. The 1851 painting *Washington Crossing the Delaware* by Emanuel Leutze is in the public domain because its copyright has expired. The painting is in the collection of New York's Metropolitan Museum of Art; the image is courtesy Google Art Project. The image has been cropped.

11. The 1914 photograph from the Christmas Truce is in the public domain because its copyright has expired. The photographer and source is unknown.

12. The illustration of Sir Isaac Newton is a copy of a painting by Sir Gordon Kneller, and first appeared in the 1917 book *A Temple of Worthies* by Arthur Shuster and Arthur Shipley. It is in the public domain because its copyright has expired.

13. The photograph of Louis Chevrolet was taken in the 1920s. It is form the George Grantham Bain Collection at the Library of Congress (digital ID ggbain.22926). According to the Library, there are no known copyright restrictions on the use of this work.

14. The 1959 CBS publicity photograph of Rod Serling by Gabor Rona is in the public domain because it was first published in the United States between 1923 and 1977 without a copyright notice. Traditionally, publicity photographs are not copyrighted because of the way in which they are intended to be used.

15. The copyright status of the August 1944 edition of *Believe It or Not!* is unknown, but it is presumed to be under copyright. Its use here is under "fair use" provisions of the copyright code. It is used to illustrate an important historical figure, no free media equivalent is available, and it is

printed in a small size and low resolution version making it unsuitable for the production of counterfeit goods. No challenge to the copyright status of the image is intended or implied.

16. The publicity photograph of Humphrey Bogart is in the public domain because it was first published in the United States between 1923 and 1963. It is unclear whether the image was originally copyrighted, but the copyright was not renewed and the image is therefore in the public domain.

17. The 1980 photograph of Anwar Sadat was taken by either Warren K. Leffler or Marion S. Trikosko, staff photographers for *US News and World Report*. The image is from the *US News and World Report* Collection at the Library of Congress (digital ID ppmsca.09814), and per the deed of gift, US News and World Reports dedicated to the public all rights it held in this photograph.

18. The 1865 photograph of Clara Barton was taken by Mathew Brady, and is in the public domain because its copyright has expired. The image is from the US National Archives and Records Administration, ARC Identifier 526057.

19. The 1947 photograph of Cab Calloway is by William P. Gottlieb, and is from the William P. Gottlieb Collection at the Library of Congress (LC-GLB13-0095). In accordance with the wishes of William Gottlieb, the photographs in this collection entered into the public domain on February 16, 2010.

20. The photograph of Evelyn Nesbit was taken circa 1900 by Gertrude Käsebier, and is in the public domain because its copyright has expired. It is courtesy of the Library of Congress, digital ID ppmsca.12056.

21. The 1974 photograph of Jairzinho was taken by Rob Mieremet and is courtesy of the Dutch National Archives and Spaarnestad Photo, CC BY-SA 3.0 Netherlands.

22. The 1887 Goodwin & Co. baseball card of Pud Galvin is in the public domain because its copyright has expired.

23. The 1918 publicity photograph of Charlie Chaplin from the film *A Dog's Life* is in the public domain because it was first published in the United States before January 1, 1923.

24. The photograph of W. C. Fields from the 1935 film *David Copperfield* is in the public domain because it was published in the United States between 1923 and 1963 and although there may or may not have been a copyright notice, the copyright was not renewed.

25. The photograph of Old and Young Tom Morris by Thomas Rodger was taken in the 1870s, and is in the public domain because its copyright has expired.

26. The 1879 drawing of the Sol Invictus temple in Rome is by Hermann Bender. It is in the public domain because its copyright has expired.

27. The artist who created the 19th century painting of a Hanukkah celebration is unknown. The image is in the public domain because its copyright has expired.

28. The photograph of a bingo card was taken by Abbey Hendrickson, and is used here under CC BY-SA 2.0. It has been cropped.

29. The 1876 Currier & Ives "Merry Christmas" card is in the public domain because its copyright has expired. It is courtesy of the Library of Congress Prints and Photographs Collection, digital ID cph.3a05129.

30. The 1815 woodcut of a proposal is in the public domain because its copyright has expired.

31. The painting "December" is from the *Brevarium Grimani,* circa 1510, and is in the public domain because its copyright has expired.

32. The etching "December" by Gabriel Perrelle was created circa 1660 and is in the public domain because its copyright has expired. The image is courtesy Wellcome Images, ICV No. 7850 BR, photo V0007629EBR, and is used here under CC BY-SA 4.0.

33. The 1815 woodcut of a proposal is in the public domain because its copyright has expired.

34. The 16th century oil on lapis lazuli painting *Perseus Rescuing Andromeda* is by Giuseppe Cesari. It is in the public domain because its copyright has expired. The original object is in the collection of the Saint Louis Art Museum.

35. The 1882 painting of *Ilex aquifolium* (holly) is by Anton Hartinger, and appeared originally in the book *Atlas der Alpenflora*.

36. The celestial sphere is from *Scenography of the Ptolemaic Cosmography*, by Johannes van Loon, based on Andreas Cellarius's *Harmonia Macrocosmica*, 1660. It is in the public domain because its copyright has expired.

37. The 1906 automobile calendar is by Edward Penfield, and is in the collection of the Library of Congress Prints and Photographs Division. It is in the public domain because its copyright has expired.

38. The 50-year perpetual calendar photograph is in the public domain.

39. The cartoon by John T. McCutcheon is from his 1905 collection *The Mysterious Stranger and Other Cartoons by John T. McCutcheon*. It is in the public domain because its copyright has expired.

40. The 1896 drawing "December" by Eugène Grasset is in the public domain because its copyright has expired.

Timespinner
Press

License Description and Terms

Aside from material purely in the public domain, photographs and other material in this book are used under specific licenses permitting free use, usually with an attribution requirement. For full text and terms of these licenses, click or enter the appropriate links below. If you believe there is an error in the copyright status or attribution of any of these images, please email us.

- Creative Commons Attribution 2.0 Generic (CC-BY 2.0): http://creativecommons.org/licenses/by/2.0/deed.en
- Creative Commons Attribution-Share Alike 3.0 Generic (CC-BY-SA 3.0): http://creativecommons.org/licenses/by-sa/3.0/
- Creative Commons Attribution-Share Alike 2.5 Generic (CC-BY-SA 2.5): http://creativecommons.org/licenses/by-sa/2.5/deed.en
- Creative Commons Attribution-Share Alike 2.0 Generic (CC-BY-SA 2.0): http://creativecommons.org/licenses/by/2.0/deed.en
- Creative Commons Attribution-Share Alike 1.0 Generic (CC-BY-SA 1.0): http://creativecommons.org/licenses/by-sa/1.0/deed.en
- CC0 1.0 Universal (CC0 1.0) Public Domain Dedication (CC0 1.0) http://creativecommons.org/publicdomain/zero/1.0/deed.en
- GNU Free Documentation License (GFDL): http://en.wikipedia.org/wiki/Wikipedia:Text_of_the_GNU_Free_Documentation_License
- License Art Libre (Free Art License): http://artlibre.org

"December" by Eugène Grasset

Other Books from Timespinner Press

The Story of a Special Day
Michael Dobson

A series of (eventually) 366 volumes covering everything that happened on your special day! Events, births, deaths, quotes, holidays, and much more. It's like a birthday card they'll never throw away!

US$7.95 print/US$2.99 ebook.

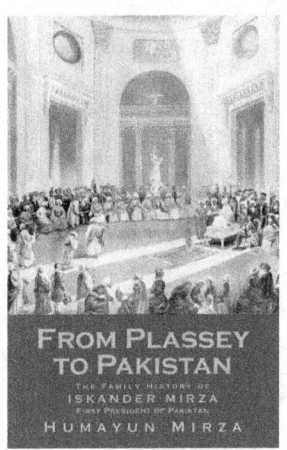

From Plassey to Pakistan
Humayun Mirza

The history of British Colonial India and the formation of Pakistan from the unique perspective of the son of Pakistan's first president and last of the royal line of Bengal, Bihar, and Orissa! This unique historical document tells the inside story of this distinguished family, including the detailed story of the coup that toppled his father from power!

US$27.95 print

A Whole New Navy: America's War in the Pacific

Miles Durr

The most comprehensive and detailed description of America's naval war in the Pacific ever—every battle, every ship, every task force and every task group from Pearl Harbor through the Japanese surrender! A must-have for the collection of every World War II buff!

US$29.95 print

Improbable History: The Weird, the Obscure, and the Strangely Important

edited by Michael Dobson

From the birth of Western civilization to the rescue of Apollo 13, from the Leaning Tower of Pisa to Florence's Duomo, history has often turned on small, improbable details. Whatever happened to the ancient Samaritan people? Why did a fortuitous rainstorm allow the British to conquer India? How did an air raid in Italy lead to the development of chemotherapy? What happened when Albert Einstein met Adolf Hitler on the streets of Berlin? How did the Japanese manage to attack the US mainland using balloons? A cast of award-winning writers tackle some of the strangest tales in history!

US$19.95 print